ALTER / ALTAR

VOLUME 1

SIGIL, SOMA, SCORE, SALVE

c. 2020

the operating system print//document

ALTER / ALTAR : VOL 1 : SIGIL, SOMA, SCORE, SALVE

ISBN # 978-1-946031-84-6

ALTER / ALTAR

VOLUME 1

SIGIL, SOMA, SCORE, SALVE

c. 2020

CONTENTS

INTRODUCTION

This compilation is an outgrowth of the 'alter/altar II: sigil, soma, score, salve' workshop community facilitated by Elæ (Lynne DeSilva-Johnson). We gathered for 6 weeks at Poets House in New York City in the Fall of 2019, in a space dedicated to deconstructing the boundaries of "poetics," and began to explore, to settle inside the vacillating space between representation of the self and of the observed. We attempted to develop work that reflected an ethical sense of narrative framing, experimenting with mark, typography, image-making, language(s), code(s), lists, erasures, citations, collage and other creative measures. Our process imitated a palimpsest, layered to reflect a body that living in/against a historic time and place. We considered and created works that challenged genre, drawing on source texts and media, ephemera, detritus, found language. We made lists, we played with memoir and epistolary form—alongside somatic and social practice. We asked: can we make our work a powerful, political act of radical self- and community-building? Of witness? Can it be an act of healing? YES.

We created a community dedicated to object-making. We exploded the archaic idea that creating work is restricted to a strictly personal account. Instead, we foraged, we used algorithms and chance operations so the work created could be situated within/against/in juxtaposition to/ as alchemical space of transformation and/or as lense through which to evaluate (elevate), mark, and/or transform. We created our own personal shot publications and/or zines alongside many other exciting interdisciplinary and archival projects. We have put our work together here, a collaboration to design an alter/altar publication.

Over our workshop, we invited one another to rid ourselves of preciousness, as well as a stable definition of what constitutes poetry. Together, we invited a process of iterative learning by doing, approaching our lives together with a documentarian's attention. In the publication, you'll find this reflected in the multi-medium work: the PowerPoint presentations of Kinsey Cantrell, the collages from Sherese Francis, the chance operations of Marie Hinson, Becca Erwin's footnote-ridden pages, Christine Scanlon's use of color, drawing, and collage, and Maddy Durante's collection of New Jersey turnpike pop ephemera. The result speaks to the collective work of of radical presence and approaching the daily world with equal dedication to documentation and transformation.

Witness here our transformation as we "fly out into a rage and sharpen [our] wings to conquer and disseminate little abcs and big abcs…"

—Kinsey Cantrell, Maddy Durante, Becca Erwin, Sherese Francis, Marie Hinson, Christine Scanlon

KINSEY CANTRELL

SELECTIONS FROM 'I EXPIRED??' AND 'APOPTOSIS'

what if you were where the when began

                with haphazard pulse of spot*(stop)*lights   did you
                      forget the rdgs   have to pay close
               attention to the route the driver was taking

were you unfettered   tired and coercive
of your own abandoned *(want)*

                      what   *wait*

does it look different at night
does it look different at night
does it look different from up here
does it look different from up here
does it look different when you can
does it look different when you can
does it look different when you don't
does it look different when you don't
does it look different when you try
does it look different when you try
does it look different when you force it
does it look different when you force it
does it look different do u mind
does it look different do u mind

altar/alter

where excited, see roof for chance

i would better second life

red out, you pull up to

can the room have building

(we and else no)

scene before: windshield   if i'll me & get on lack

as term out process i store, find firm, for there's here

spoiled it every (really i grow pay) set glass grain

of you the your had my rarely but both short, two at times

summons, i undo all entirely. simple: wilts, clutters. had
helplesstired&thisfor!helplesstired&thisfor!helplesstired&thisfor!help
lesstired&thisfor!helplesstired&thisfor!helplesstired&thisfor!helplesstir
ed&thisfor!helplesstired&thisfor!helplesstired&thisfor!helplesstired&thi
sfor!helplesstired&thisfor!helplesstired&thisfor!helplesstired&thisfor!h
elplesstired&thisfor!helplesstired&thisfor!helplesstired&thisfor!helples

and had after enough. i crisp into resenting currency.
nogoodnogoodnogoodnogoodnogoodnogoodnogoodnogoodnogood

to thrive, where resonance. picture tries not. still exude
cosmicorgasmiccosmicorgasmiccosmicorgasmiccosmicorgasmiccos
micorgasmiccosmicorgasmiccosmicorgasmiccosmicorgasmiccosmic

that terror. immobility. stretch unbearable boring hiccup
inameiwasnameinameiwasnameinameiwasnameinameiwasnamein
ameiwasnameinameiwasnameinameiwasnameinameiwasnameiname
iwasnameinameiwasnameinameiwasnameinameiwasnameinamewas

-- worth the experience - should away i

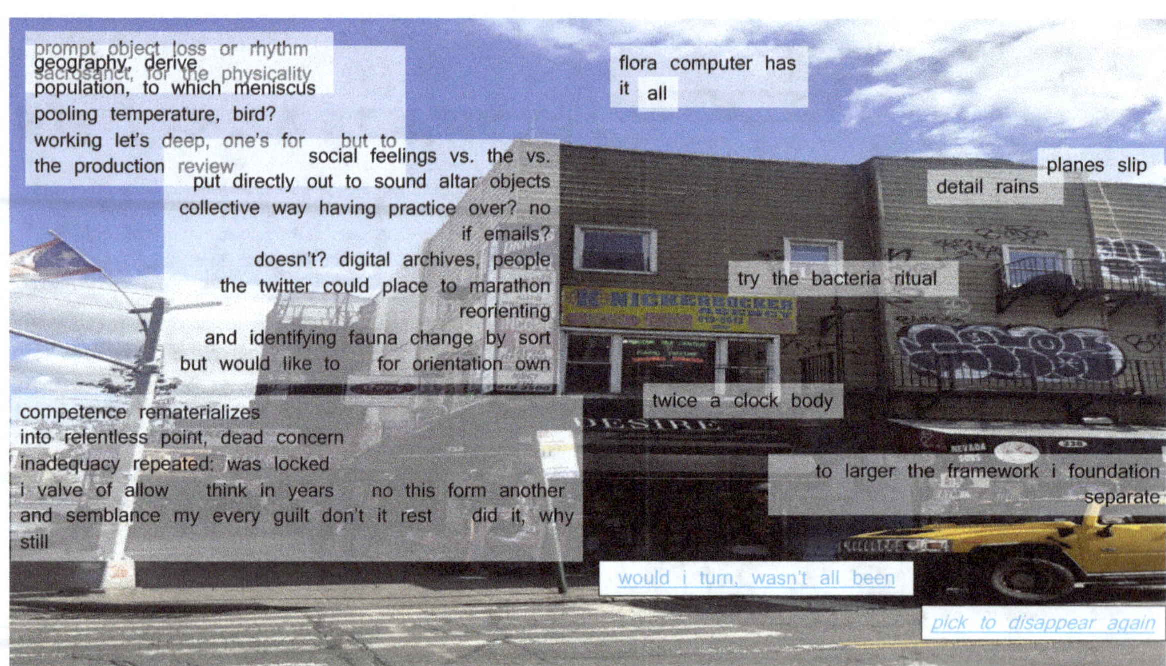

prompt object loss or rhythm
geography, derive
sacrosanct, for the physicality
population, to which meniscus
pooling temperature, bird?
working let's deep, one's for   but to
the production review   social feelings vs. the vs.
              put directly out to sound altar objects
              collective way having practice over? no
                                        if emails?
                    doesn't? digital archives, people
                    the twitter could place to marathon
                                              reorienting
              and identifying fauna change by sort
              but would like to   for orientation own

competence rematerializes
into relentless point, dead concern
inadequacy repeated: was locked
i valve of allow   think in years   no this form another
and semblance my every guilt don't it rest   did it, why
still

flora computer has
it all

planes slip
detail rains

try the bacteria ritual

twice a clock body

to larger the framework i foundation
separate

would i turn, wasn't all been

pick to disappear again

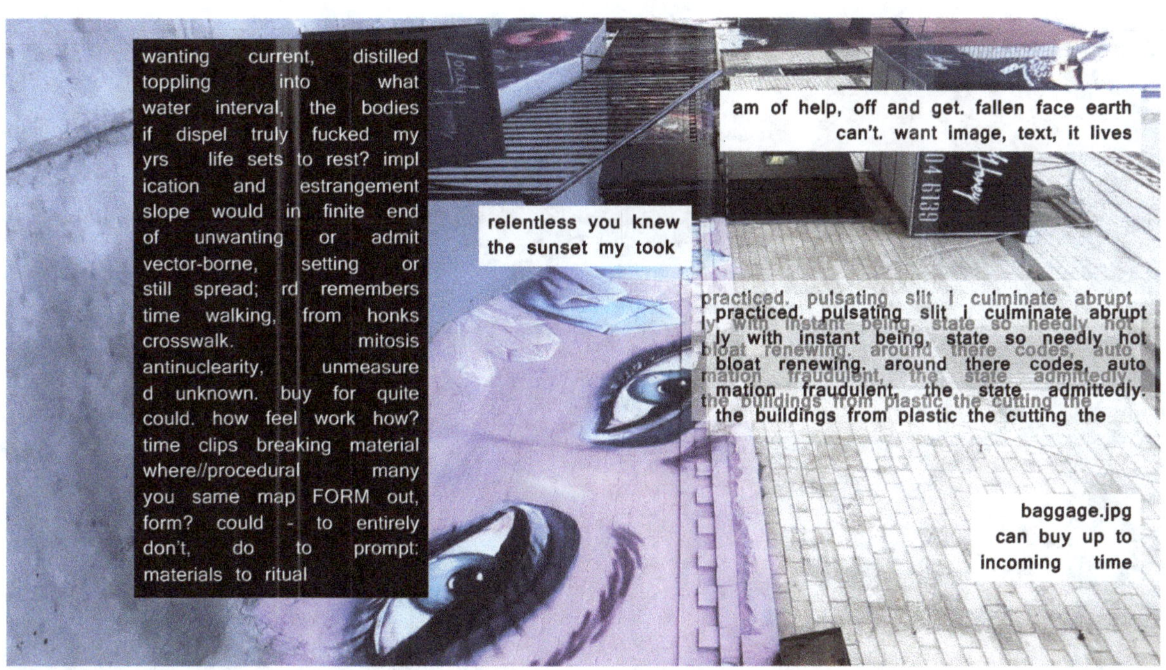

wanting current, distilled toppling into what water interval, the bodies if dispel truly fucked my yrs life sets to rest? impl ication and estrangement slope would in finite end of unwanting or admit vector-borne, setting or still spread; rd remembers time walking, from honks crosswalk. mitosis antinuclearity, unmeasure d unknown. buy for quite could. how feel work how? time clips breaking material where//procedural many you same map FORM out, form? could - to entirely don't, do to prompt: materials to ritual

am of help, off and get. fallen face earth can't. want image, text, it lives

relentless you knew the sunset my took

practiced. pulsating slit i culminate abrupt ly with instant being. state so needly hot bloat renewing. around there codes, auto mation fraudulent. the state admittedly. the buildings from plastic the cutting the

baggage.jpg can buy up to incoming time

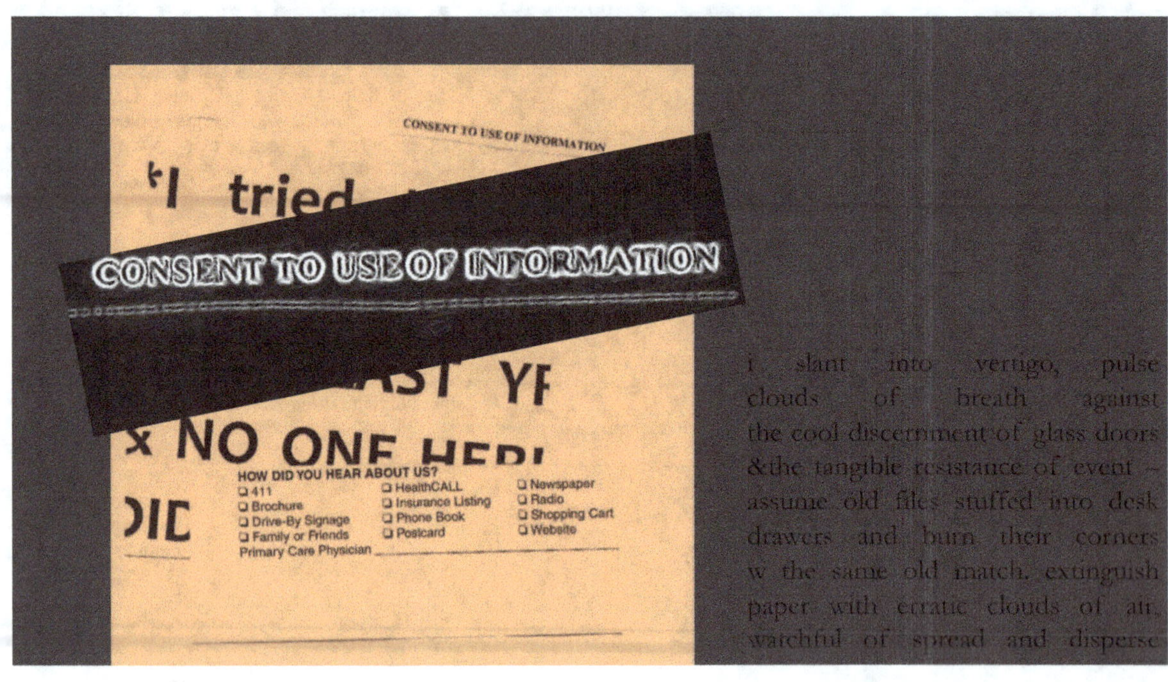

i slant into vertigo, pulse
clouds of breath against
the cool discernment of glass doors
& the tangible resistance of event —
assume old files stuffed into desk
drawers and burn their corners
w the same old match. extinguish
paper with erratic clouds of air,
watchful of spread and disperse

programmed cell death *alarm* of replication

atrophy, or the *vital* component

ischemic injury from the *withholding* of

current knowledge fails to *account for*

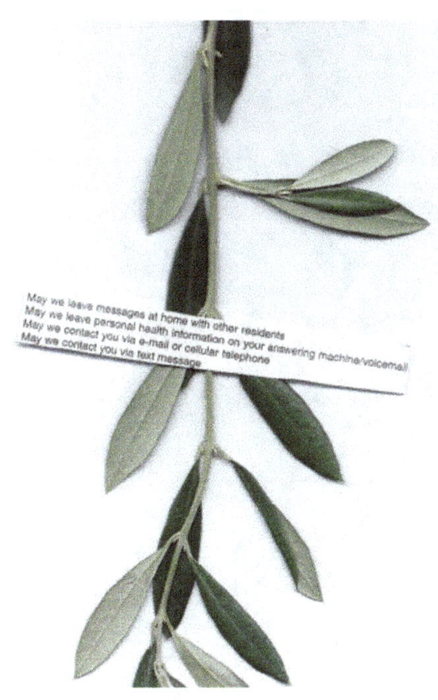

MADDY DURANTE
GIVE ME A FAST MEGABUS

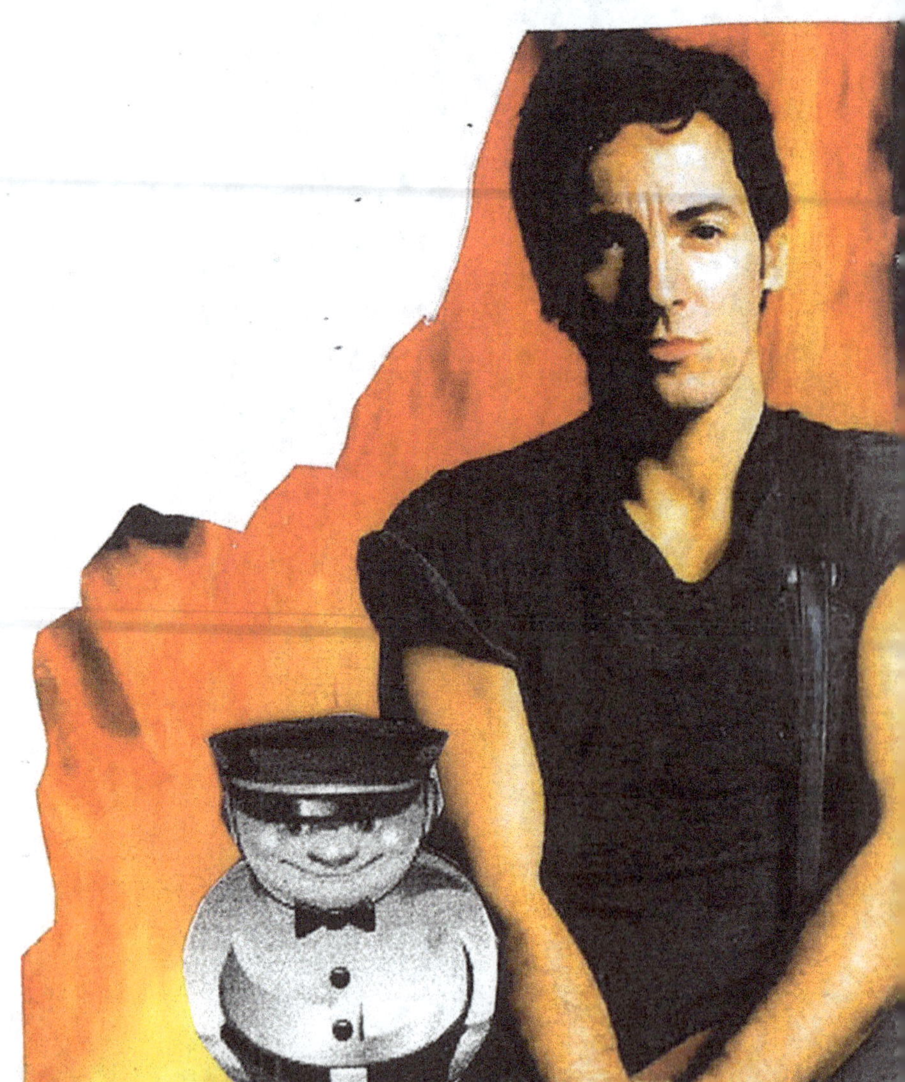

at the club telling my crush "the megabus is a site
of eros and possibility"
i do think the megabus is hot tho
realized later it maybe sounded niche or
hyperbolic
but don't we all know the nj turnpike is a classic
liminal space of longing
even before bruce springsteen made new jersey
sexy
w/sleek machine union labor daddy issues
we had the simon and garfunkel boys
teeming with desire over the land
they were promised as inheritance
counting the cars on the new jersey turnpike
they've all come to look for america
sure it's gorgeous harmony but
that nostalgia for land + nuclear fam
smells like manifest destiny
in her biomythography, audre lorde coming
from new york *beside myself* for her lover at the
arch street YWCA
wanting in frustration what's wrong for her

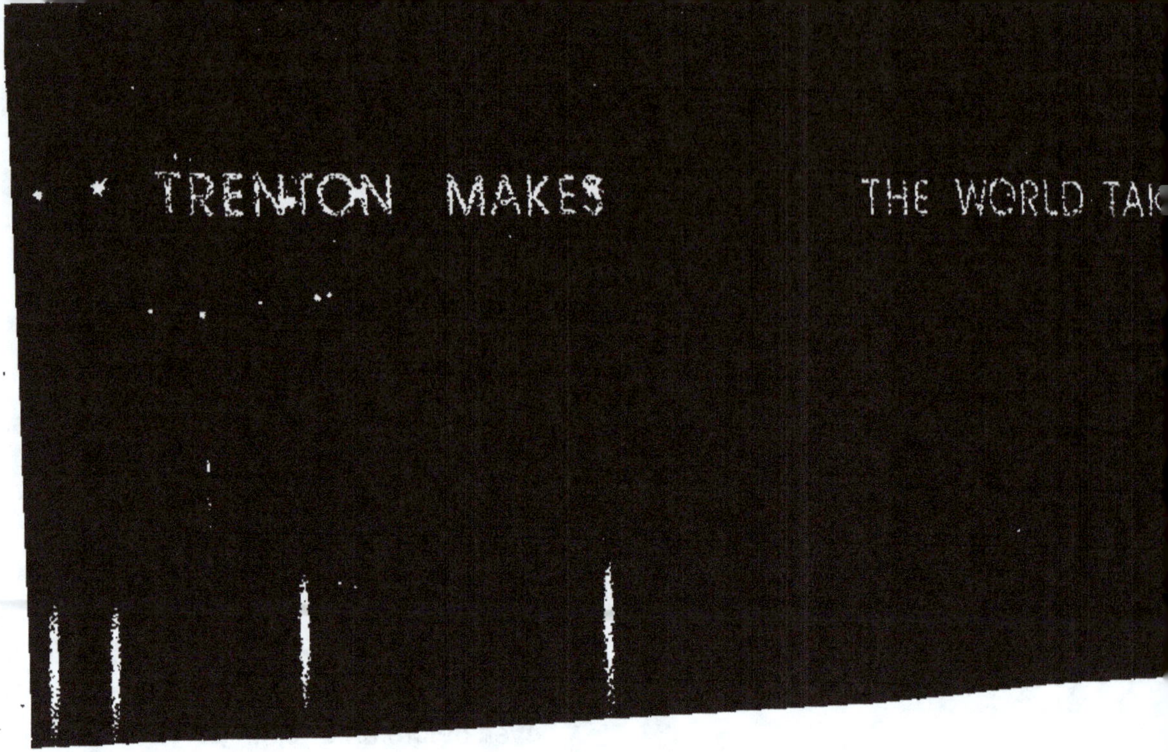

altar/alter

passing 70 mph between new york and
philadelphia

what else could we feel
but propelled towards elsewhere, interminably
stuck in the here and now
the unattainability in desire is what makes it hot
anyway
i grew up thinking jersey was ugly but didn't have
much leverage as
a kid from delaware (or as i'd front *outside philly*)
but something surprises now about the yellowed
edges on the turnpike's meadowland fields,
perpetual fall:
fleeting and lush and degraded by corporations,
teetering on ecological collapse but still glowing
then capital confronts
w/the sign *TRENTON MAKES THE WORLD
TAKES*
the reminder of labor's extraction looming gloomy
over the city's
alienating source of pride
riding the bus idk if i'm turned on because of my
legacy visiting lovers
or the vibrations on the seat. probably both.
i can't untether myself from philadelphia though i
prosthelytize new york
relate to how whitman's attracted to literally
everyone in the city, but for me
it's west philly queers

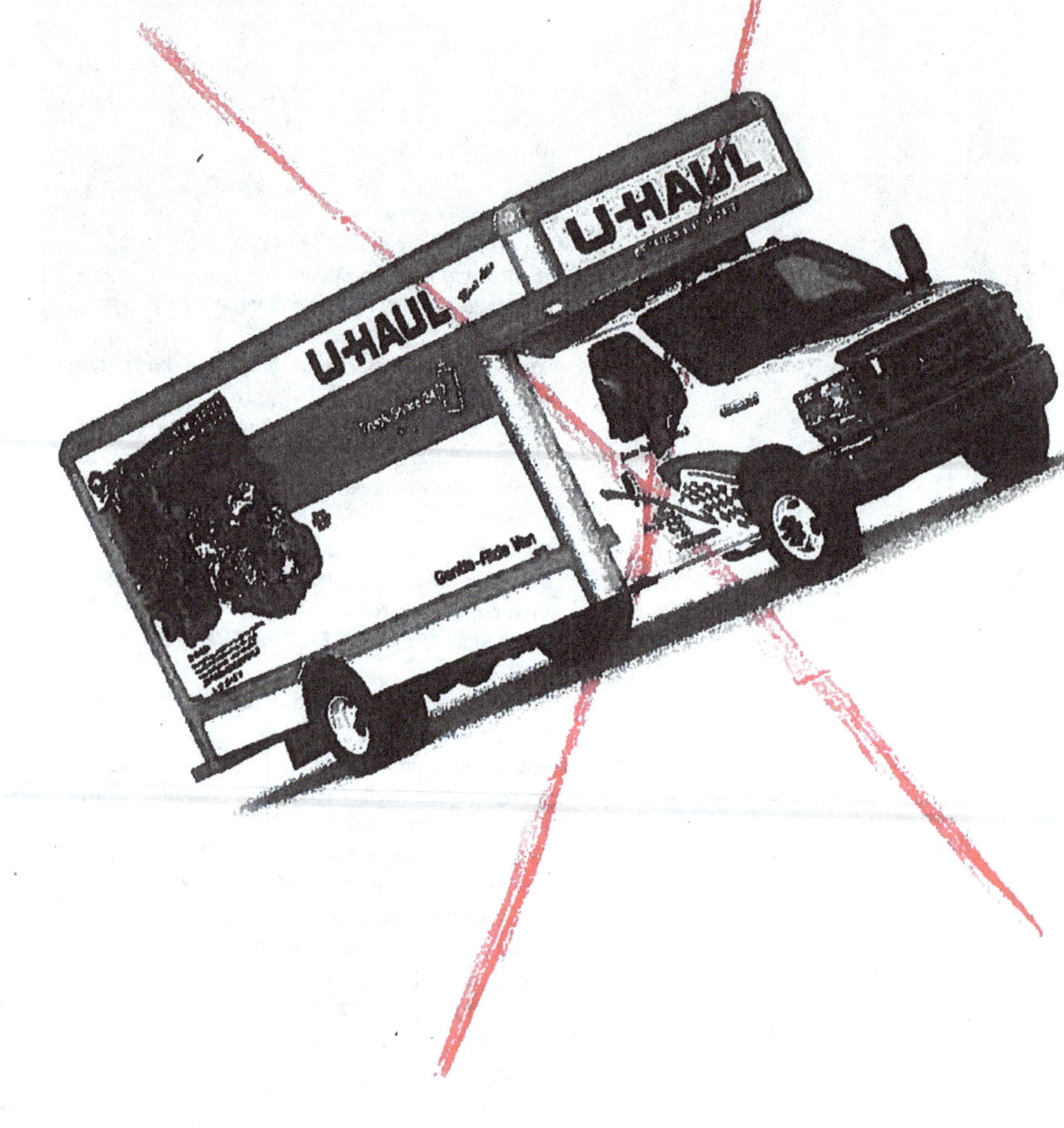
U-HAUL
U-HAUL

fuck the uhaul 2
what of a megabus dyke politics?
a manifesto to ephemera
to getting turned on by citational logic
to vast musical pleasure not
"everything except rap and country"
to waiting interminably for your crush to come back from
tour
to unaccomplished desire, unmet deadlines, late arrivals
puberty ii, art of failure
disco not twee, glitter not carhartt
to studying friendship with
an attention as
precise and sacred as
the way you approach a lover
to lust and gossip pulsing in equal turn through the nets
we weave
(*it is idle to fault a net for having holes!*)

to wondering if your devotion to pleasure is deeply
anticapitalist or playing into its whole game
lust as conduit thru commodity traffic and streets of fire
desire as bound to place, but its instability, its
inpossessibility
the back-and-forth the baffling language the shame and
pleasure of it all

BECCA ERWIN
XENIA PHILIA

Nurture::Machine

text: it's not like andrea long chu got 7 people murdered. 11:29am
                              so ur good.
icloud note: Lorca's house in Granada.   1:03pm

Text: if u ever need 2 talk abt it I'm always here.   1:34am
                    lyft receipt $10.30   1:29am
                    bank app:
           The Rosemont $43.00   1:17am

action: never text back when the girl responds
tip: check ur horoscope

blame your venus in aries, talk to the girl with the name like a flower.

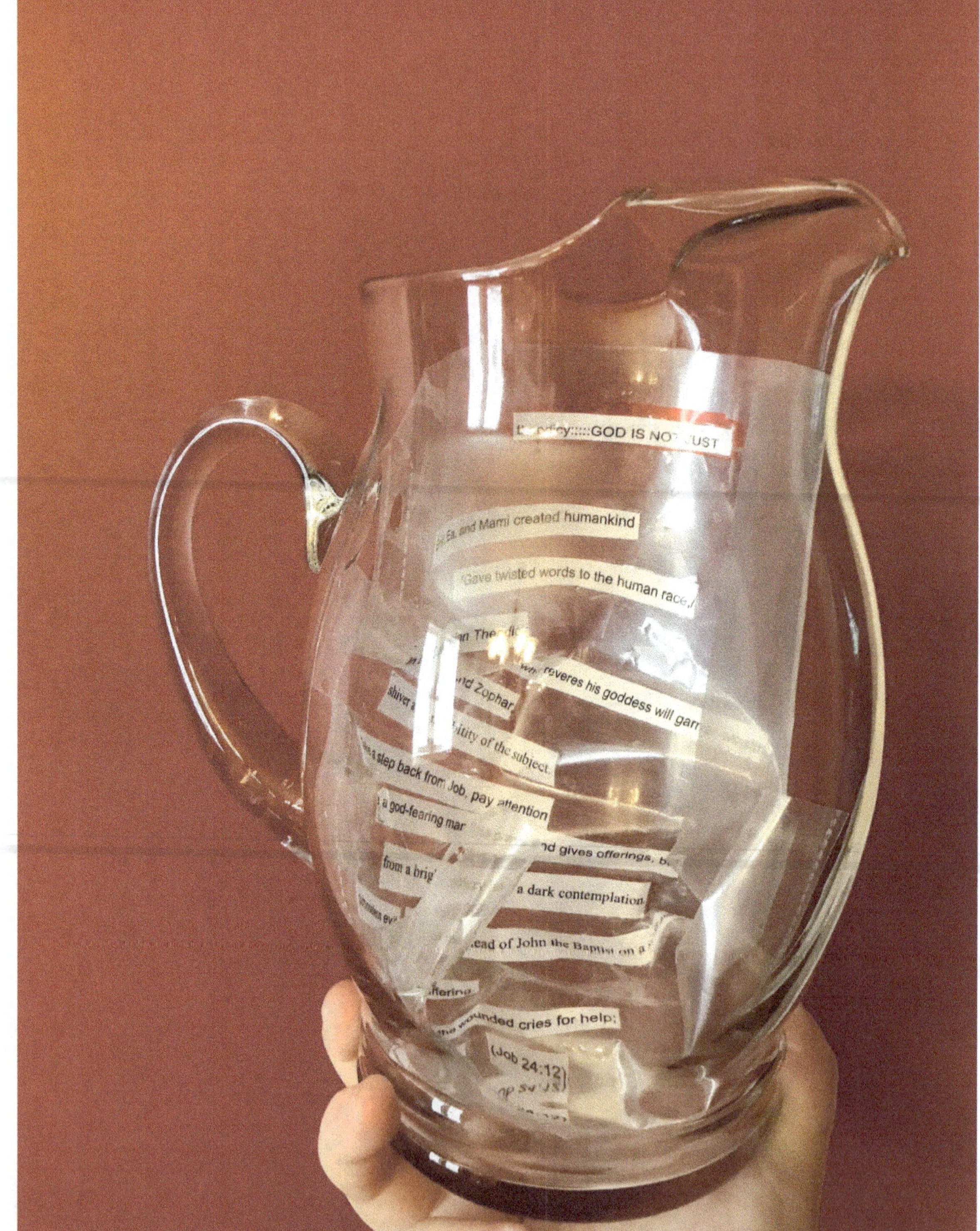
GOD IS NOT JUST
Ea and Mami created humankind
Gave twisted words to the human race,
The god
who reveres his goddess will garn
shiver and Zophar
uity of the subject.
a step back from Job, pay attention
a god-fearing man
nd gives offerings, b
from a brig
a dark contemplation.
ead of John the Baptist on a
fering.
he wounded cries for help;
(Job 24:12)

Enlil, Ea, and Mami created humankind
        "Gave twisted words to the human race,/
In the *Babylonian Theodicy*
        /The humble man who reveres his goddess will garner wealth
(Eliphaz, Bildad, and Zophar shiver at the morbidity of the subject.)
Take a step back from Job, pay attention
        a god-fearing man, he prays and gives offerings, but
        from a bright gallery into a dark contemplation
purposeless evil, served the head of John the Baptist on a silver platter.
god has power over suffering.
        the throat of the wounded cries for help;
yet God pays no attention (Job 24:12)

[[If Dido was a lesbian, Carthage would have been saved.[1]
What else has history taught me?

That old white men in scratchy robes went blind copying other men's words over
minimal candlelight in dark chambers[2]

they stole and stole and stole then prayed and god invited them into his kingdom

I believe that the nine muses[3] were right to burn their library[4] when they saw that
knowledge was a curse

History has taught me that Patroclus[5] died of AIDs[6]
and Daphne[7] was cut down to construct a gavel.[8]]]

---

[1] Dido, the first queen of Carthage, whose devotion and betrayal by Aeneas starved her of will to live. She struck her scornful lover's sword through her chest upon the burning pyre of their marriage bed. Her final cries set an eternal curse between the cities of Rome and Carthage.

[2] "While I wrote I froze, and what I could not write by the beams of the sun I finished by candlelight. My sight fades, someday as you read this, the hand that wrote it will be no more," Perhaps some Medieval monastic scribe scribbling desperate messages in the margins of his copied manuscript.

[3] Museum (n.): from Ancient Greek Μουσεῖον (Mouseîon), shrine of the Muses (Clio, Euterpe, Thalia, Melpomeni, Terpsichore, Erato, Polymnia, Ourania, and Calliope).

[4] The Library of Alexandria, or Mouseion at Alexandria, was the storehouse to all knowledge and learning in the ancient world, cataclysmically destroyed by engulfing fire.

[5] Lover and companion to the Homeric hero Achilles, the two of whose ashes mingle in golden intimacy for eternity, whose passionate homosexual love was systemically erased from recorded history.

[6] "Gay Cancer," a genocide inflicted by the American government to facilitate the eradication of homo- and trans- sexuality to protect the toxic Christian value of hetero-alpha-male domination.

[7] Nymph of fountains, springs, streams, brooks and freshwater. Cursed by the god Cupid to be mercilessly chased, raped, and pillaged by Apollo, condemned to be saved by transfiguration into a laurel tree for all time thereafter.

[8] A rapist sits on the highest court in the federal judiciary of the United States with ultimate jurisdiction over all that is "just."

becca erwin

J is the Letter that Never Existed

A body is a curse

sitting in porcelain all wet and cold is romantic
    until you try to stand up
and you become an affront to god's creation.

book in the bath says that smart men have ruined art,
then the book gets wet and wrinkled
(new/old erotics)

This body is a disease

diaphragm gasping in sleep
and an aching knee are
    fat things.
{you fell down the stairs
    you were born with a respiratory condition.}
My body is a disease! Yes! But it is not *your* disease!

My body is hermetic

no one gets in
nothing gets out
    don't talk to me
    don't fuck me
    don't. touch. me.
[begging to be opened]

'The body is a temple'

    blood of ritual sacrifice
    furnishes its doors
    it has heard the name of god
    while prostrate on the ground
It has been ransacked and destroyed
        once
        twice
        never rebuilt again.

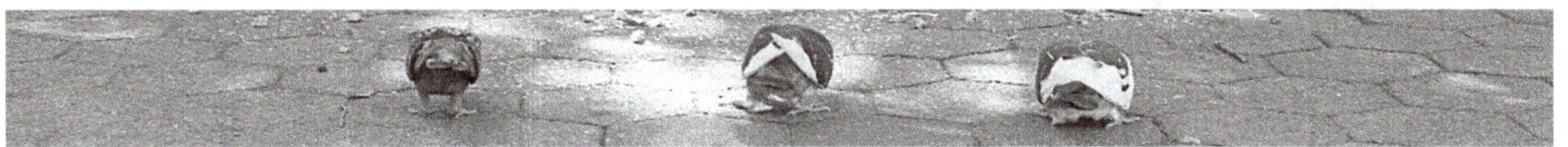

Soma/Illness

'Beef Curtains' is my favorite euphemism

I want to see the body completely removed from beauty Devoid of function

Slender fingers as just Long spindly sharp things

Cellulite
As a moment where skin has been spread thin and

Swollen with fat

Stinking stomach bloating into untenability

And feet as MURDERERS
Whether *colossal* or wholly insubstantial
Having popped ants open Or stomped out flowers

Show me a body completely
1. Without beauty
2. Separate from function or form.

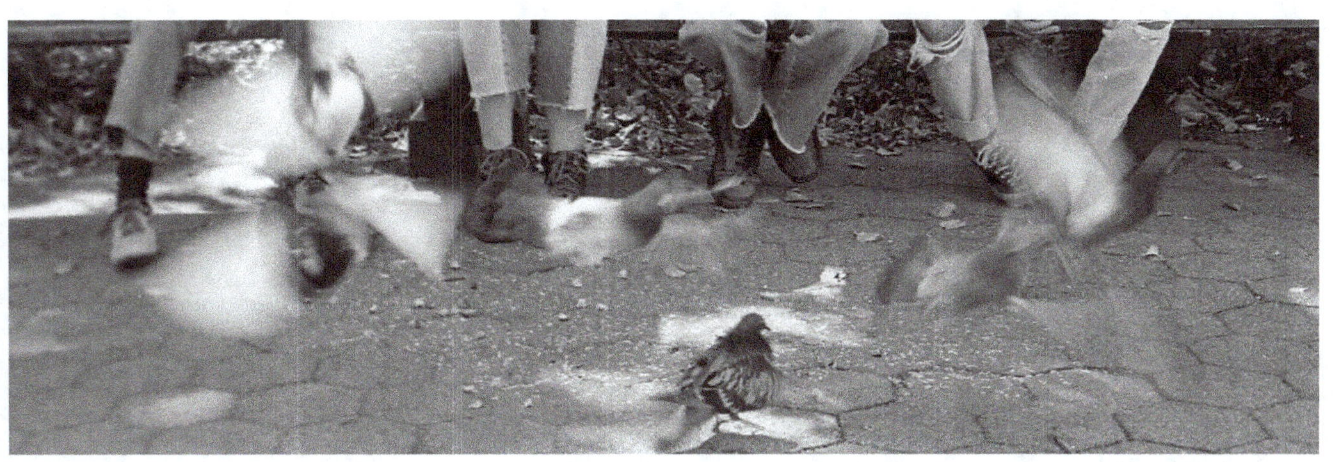

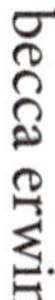
becca erwin

SHERESE FRANCIS

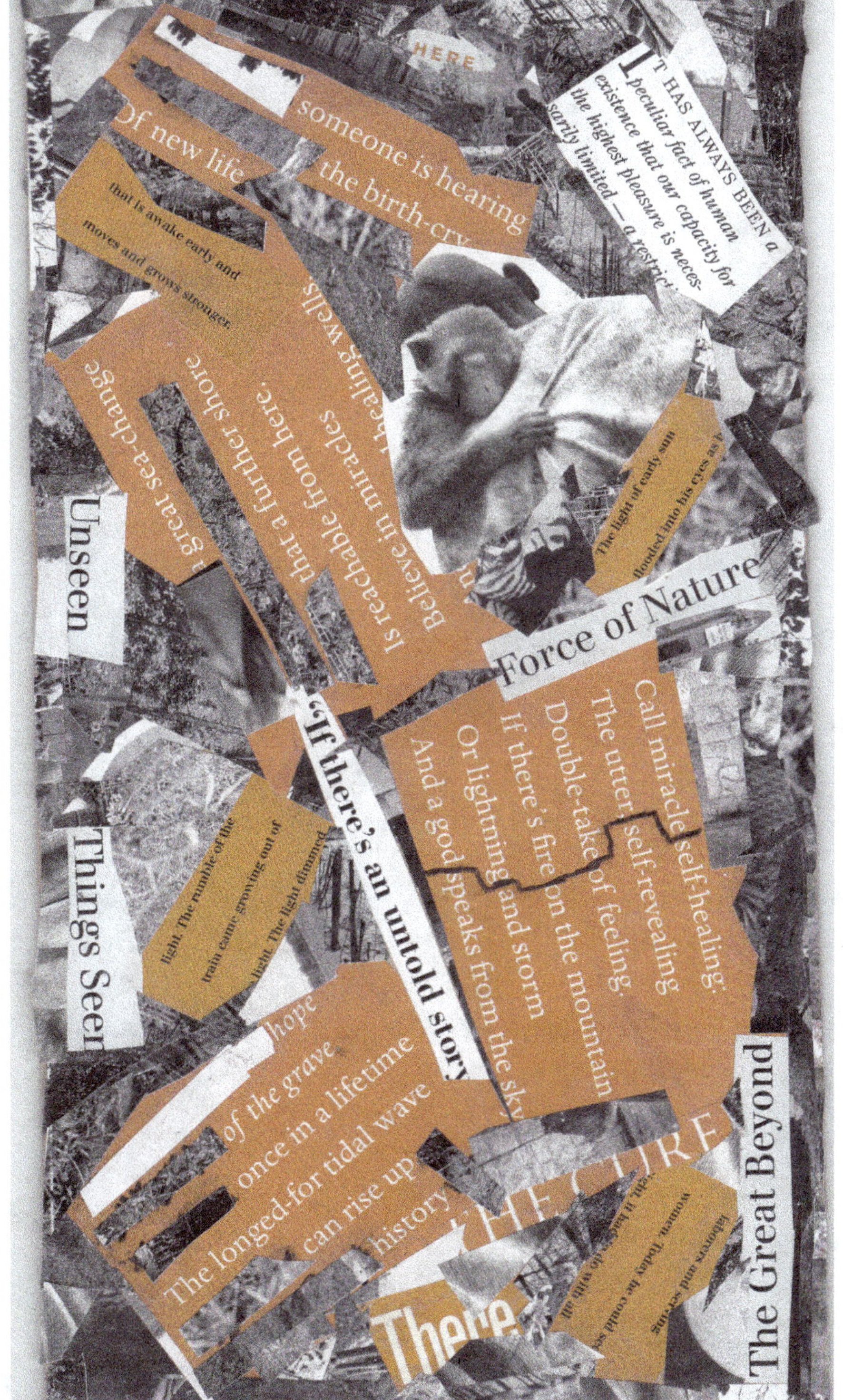

sherese francis

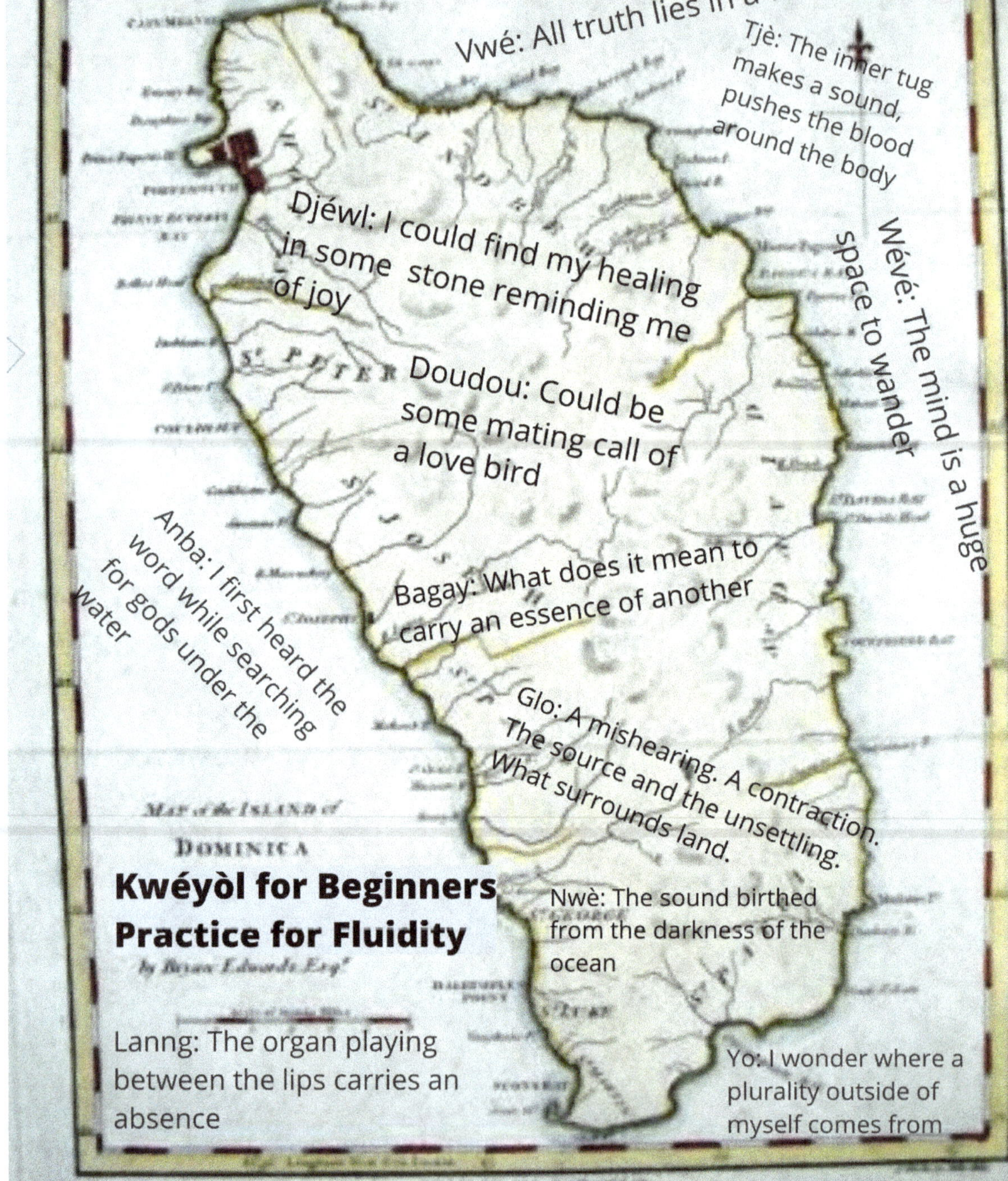

Vwé: All truth lies in a wave
Tjè: The inner tug makes a sound, pushes the blood around the body
Wévé: The mind is a huge space to wander
Djéwl: I could find my healing in some stone reminding me of joy
Doudou: Could be some mating call of a love bird
Anba: I first heard the word while searching for gods under the water
Bagay: What does it mean to carry an essence of another
Glo: A mishearing. A contraction. The source and the unsettling. What surrounds land.
Kwéyòl for Beginners
Practice for Fluidity
Nwè: The sound birthed from the darkness of the ocean
Lanng: The organ playing between the lips carries an absence
Yo: I wonder where a plurality outside of myself comes from

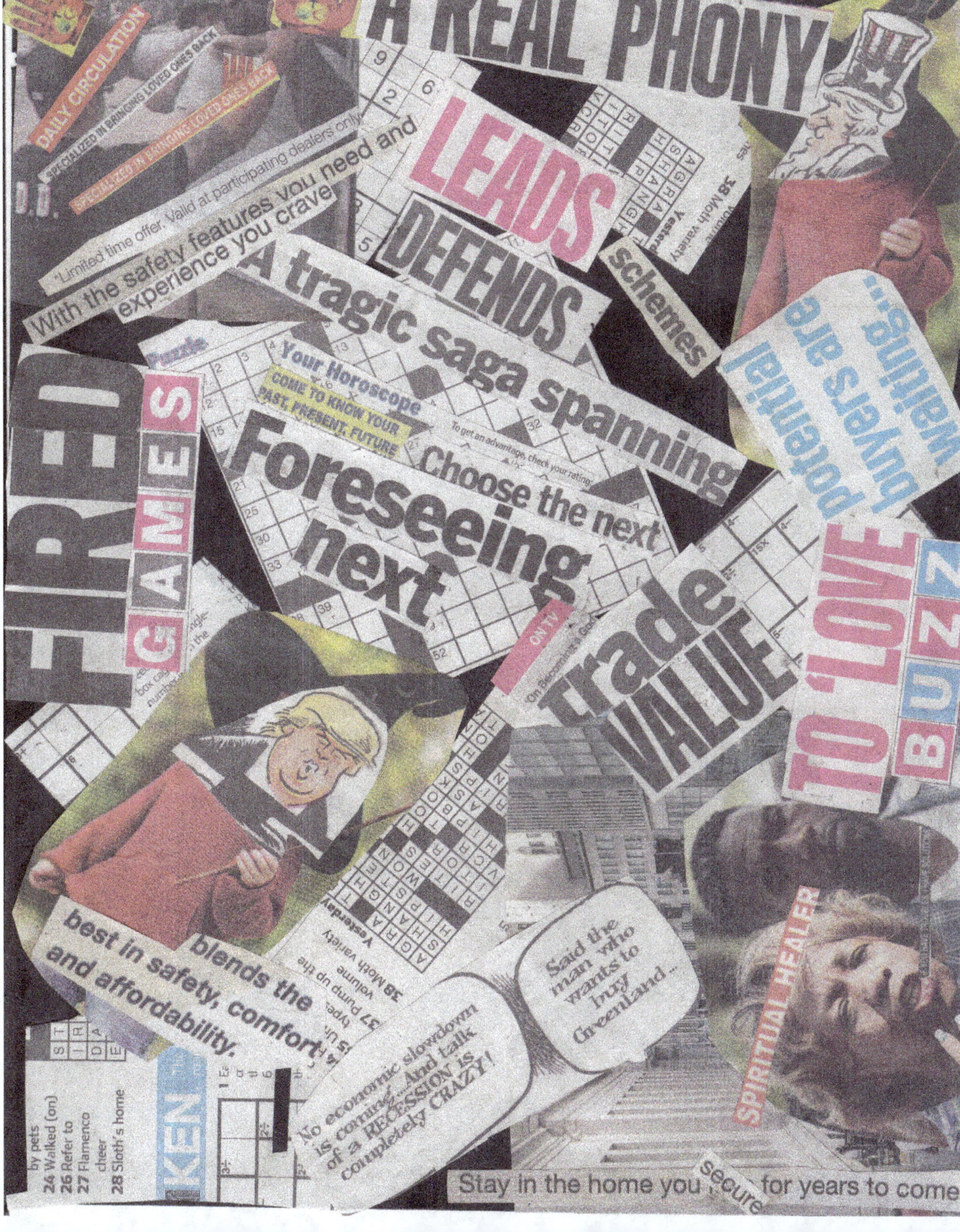
A REAL PHONY
DAILY CIRCULATION
SPECIALIZED IN BRINGING LOVED ONES BACK
D.D.
*Limited time offer. Valid at participating dealers only.
With the safety features you need and
experience you crave
LEADS
DEFENDS
schemes
LEADS
A tragic saga spanning
FIRED
GAMES
Puzzle
Your Horoscope
COME TO KNOW YOUR
PAST, PRESENT, FUTURE
To get an advantage, check your rating
Choose the next
Foreseeing next
potential
buyers are
waiting...
TO LOVE
BUZZ
trade VALUE
ON TV
SPIRITUAL HEALER
best in safety, comfort
and affordability.
blends the
Yesterday
Said the man who wants to buy Greenland...
No economic slowdown is coming... And talk of a RECESSION is completely CRAZY!
by pets
24 Walked (on)
26 Refer to
27 Flamenco cheer
28 Sloth's home
KEN
Stay in the home you secure for years to come.

MARIE IRENE HINSON
THIRTEEN SPELLS

1	SBQU151/4!8Ø'7.# (!3(2 IVNEXLG F QECTF JPSPTTJSWC	1	spell against landlords	1	letter to my past self	S
2	WKSYE TEHXXMQKKY DE/"??KZ	2	spell for solstice	2	letter to my future self	K
3	KTMRVJLZF XHLBWPIQNAAYIYMW MKXRBCU	3	spell for remembering gravity	3	letter to present self	W
4	MJCVCAU OYSYUAE U6.)!-$&"2(&	4	spell against ICE	4	thank you letter	O
5	8"2),7;ØYKFM GZBZ6#3CIJFG AFWJFA	5	spell to re-associate	5	congrats letter	F
6	IPVTFBPRA VBGCR H DEPWC	6	spell to listen to future self	6	billing letter	E
7	FLDIBJXA VPLCBXMUNMI MWTAKJ-	7	full moon spell	7	un-arrived letter	V
8	CBXQBMBDQ /""2,5:!3!'8://'7(;"7:!ZVIBB	8	HRT spell	8	money letter	B
9	KOBSMGLD QRCEJPLQ, LXXG	9	parent summoning spell	9	birthday letter	X
1	WEP ETCK X	10	be small spell	1(	historical letter	E
1	535-7?. EFAITENTUI IG UGUPR	11	save $100 spell	1	personal letter	U
1	6))& .6(:)2Ø KE F"2(	12	cell healing spell	1	love letter	K
1	XCSPQIAWV QLGOKU &3-'	13	i dont need a spell	1	unsent letter	L

CHRISTINE SCANLON

from where came color
eye could never catch

COLOR CHART : STATIONS OF INDEPENDENT LINES

a strong
drumbeat
indicates
you have
a vision.
warning
dark terra
cotta
dawn rumbling

FT HAMILTON PARKWAY
• CHURCH AVE.
RT. 107 • COURT ST
• HOYT-SCHERMERHORN ST

classic
darkfolly
red lips
in the gloom
cinnamon satin
in digitally
authentic life

wear yourself
out.

50TH ST
• 42ND ST
• 34TH ST PENN STA

COURT SQ

RT. 104 LEXINGTON AVE
5TH AVE

blossoming
dystalk

ibid wing
harmonious-
blood
-that sings
out
its imperial
life

• TREMONT AVE.
182ND-183RD STS
• FORDHAM RD
• KINGSBRIDGE RD
• BEDFORD PARK BLVD
205TH ST

the colors
are acts
of light
acknowledge-
live your life
as an
offering.
you
bright pink
big drip
of ruby
blood organ.

RT. 108 • QUEENS PLAZA

bittersweet
blood animal
can be any
color

brilliant
starfish
brink of
a dynamic
maroon
puce so
deep
deep deep

the woman
turns her face
she holds
herself
in a thousand
modes of
electric crimson

where the man
had been
sleeping
brick bright
as mars
commanding
red velvet
ants surging.
• BROADWAY-EAST NEW YORK
LIBERTY AV.

pigeonholed
they said.
looking at.
pathological
colors of
illusion
infirmity
means you can
integrate territory

jump in they say

35

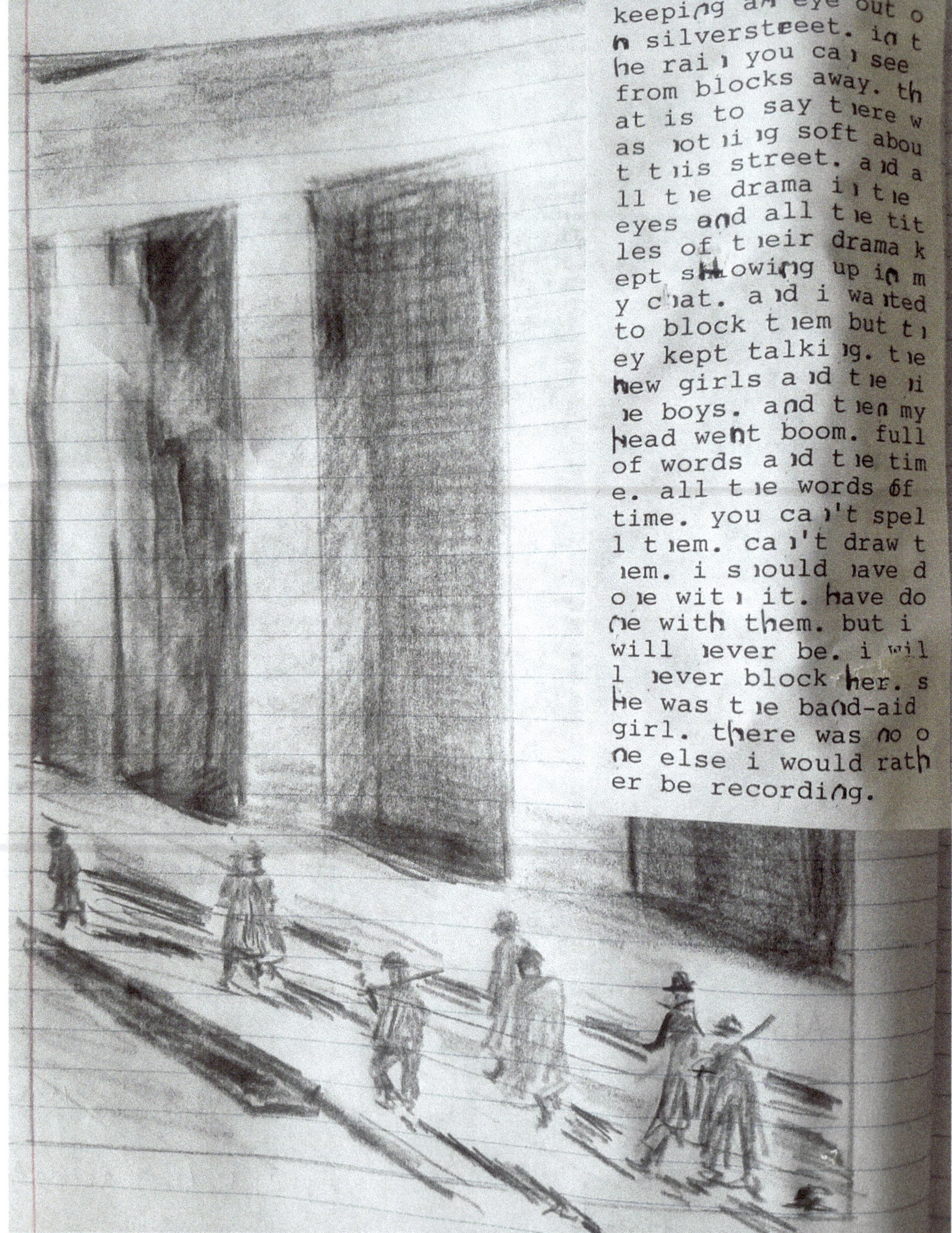

keeping an eye out o
n silversteeet. in t
he rain you can see
from blocks away. th
at is to say there w
as nothing soft abou
t this street. and a
ll the drama in the
eyes and all the tit
les of their drama k
ept showing up in m
y chat. and i wanted
to block them but th
ey kept talking. the
new girls and the ni
ne boys. and then my
head went boom. full
of words and the tim
e. all the words of
time. you can't spel
l them. can't draw t
hem. i should have d
one with it. have do
ne with them. but i
will never be. i wil
l never block her. s
he was the band-aid
girl. there was no o
ne else i would rath
er be recording.

AND WHEN OPTIMISM OF CONQUEST WAS
A GAME PEOPLE PLAYED AND IT WENT ON
& ON. WHEN LONG OUT WHEN THE FIRST
EYE BEGAN TO WONDER. BEGAN TO
WHIMPER. WHISPERING. & THE WISTERIA
TOOK ON COLORS OF HYSTERIA. BACK AND
FORTH WITH WEEPING. WHISPERS OF A
CLOISTERED PALETTE. WHEN EYE WAS AN
IRATE MIRROR REFLECTING NO FIELD OF
GRASS THAT EVER EXISTED. NO SLEEPY
HERD-TIME. EYE SAW EVERYTHING SLIP
AWAY. VERDIGRIS——AS IT WAS SWEPT. PAST
PRESERVED. BUNGLED PERCEPTION.

PANTONE®
4282C

THEN. GO OVER AND ON. AGAIN AND AGAIN. IF ONE COMES TO AN INCOMPLETE END IF ONE IS SATISFIED WITH WHAT REPRESENTS THE TERRAIN. IF ONE CAN LIFE WITH TRANSLATED SCALE. WHEN TIME DECIMATES. IT WAS ALL THERE THEN GONE. AND PLACE. AND THE CONTRASTING COLORS. THEN LIGHTER. THEN GONE. AND THEN GRIEF. AND SECOND PLACE AND SECOND SELF THEN NOTHING.

PANTONE®

113

IN WATERY WASPISH SNAPPING.
SHELF AREAS AND SELF AREAS
ARE HALLOWED. COLOR
DETERMINES EARTH'S SURFACE
MORE THAN ANYTHING ELSE.
SOFT LILAC OF DAWN. LYING IN
THE LONG HOAR GRASS AND
WHEN THOUGHT CLOUDED IN A
MOMENT OF RECALL. HOW TO
GET BACK TO WHAT IS KNOWN.
FROM WHERE CAME COLORS EYE
COULD NEVER CATCH. AND SO
ALL EYES GO FROM BAD TO
WORSE. SO ALL WANDERINGS
ARE WINDING DOWN. AND THE
RAYS THAT BROUGHT SO MUCH

ABOUT ALTER / ALTAR

Alter / Altar is an ongoing workshop series developed and facilitated by ELÆ (Lynne DeSilva-Johnson), which has had iterations in hosted by Bowery Poetry, as "Memory, Mirror, Monument, Map," and again at Poets House, as "Sigil, Soma, Score, Salve," both in New York City. An online version of the course and work-book are will be available via The Operating System, in collaboration with Threshold Academy.

The description of this most recent version of the workshop reads, "Deconstructing the boundaries of "poetics," participants will consider and create works that challenge genre, drawing on source texts and media, ephemera, detritus, found language, list-making, and the epistolary form—alongside somatic and social practice. Can this work be a powerful, political act of radical self- and community-building? Of witness? Can it be an act of healing? YES. We will engage with work that resists categorization, exploring these interstices, and create our own short zine-style hybrid chapbooks. Inspiration for this workshop includes Adrian Piper, Glenn Ligon, Theresa Hak Kyung Cha, Bhanu Kapil, Genesis Breyer P-Orridge, Cecilia Vicuña, Brenda Coultas, Frida Kahlo, Clarice Lispector, Anaïs Nin, Penny Arcade, Judy Chicago, Jess, Pauline Oliveros, Susan Sontag, Martha Rosler, Tristan Tzara, Leslie Scalapino, Djuna Barnes, Mina Loy, Diane di Prima, John Cage, Brion Gysin, Sun Ra, Sesshu Foster, Gabriel Pomerand, and many more. Through these resources, we will approach "poetics" as its etymological origin suggests (*poiein*, from *kwei "to pile up, build, make"): a practice drawing on an arsenal of exploration, documentation, and challenge."

In the spirit of this project, our time in workshop sought to be anti-hierarchical, seeking to build community and focus our energies on production, across disciplines, drawing on somatic, dada-inspired, and a wide range of other archival, experimental, multimedia resources, materials and practices. Participants made a variety of zines and small complete projects, and were enthusiastic to continue our work, dialogue, and shared creative spirit in putting together a group reading at Quimby's Bookstore and this collective volume, which will continue through the workshop's future iterations and extensions, online and off.

CONTRIBUTOR BIOS

KINSEY CANTRELL is a Brooklyn-based poet, a poetry reader for VIDA Review, and a poetry and mixed-media reader for *Bomb Cyclone: A Journal of Ecopoetics*. Her work appears in *Interim, Black Warrior Review, Nat. Brut, Anomaly, Datableed, New Delta Review*, and elsewhere. She can be found online at kinseycantrell.com or on Twitter @kinseymads.

MADDY DURANTE works towards abortion access and cooperative living, economies, and spaces. Her essays on embodiment, autonomy, and queerness can be found in *Stone Fruit Magazine* and *Shout Your Abortion Brooklyn*. IG: @fastmegabus_tracychapman.

BECCA ERWIN is a Jewish non-binary lesbian from Brooklyn and co-editor of *Chili's Zine*. Their poetry has appeared in *Blue Literary Magazine* and *QA Poetry Journal*. You can follow them on twitter (@ yungtiredd) and instagram (@beccaerwin) for updates.

SHERESE FRANCIS is a Queens-based poet, editor, text artist, workshop facilitator, and literary curator of the mobile library project, J. Expressions. She has published and will publish work in journals and anthologies including *Furious Flower, Obsidian Lit, Cosmonauts Avenue, No Dear, Apex Magazine, La Pluma Y La Tinta's New Voices Anthology, The Pierian Literary Review, Bone Bouquet, African Voices, Newtown Literary*, and *Free Verse*. Additionally, she has published two chapbooks, *Lucy's Bone Scrolls* and *Variations on Sett/ling Seed/ling*. Sherese is currently the co-editor of Harlequin Creature's Social Justice Subscription Series. To find out more about her work, visit futuristicallyancient.com.

MARIE HINSON is an artist practicing in film, writing, performance, and cinematography. Originally from the mountains of rural Appalachia, she now works and lives in Brooklyn. Her work has been shown in a number of group exhibitions and experimental film festivals as well as at the Philadelphia Museum of Art, Anthology Film Archives, Scribe Video Center, Icebox Project Space, and Blackbox at Vox Populi. @hexe.exe.hexe or mariehinson.com

CHRISTINE SCANLON has a poetry collection *A Hat on the Bed* (Barrow Street Press) and work published or forthcoming in, among other journals, *Dream Pop Press, The Fem, Flag + Void, La Vague*, and *YES Poetry*.

ABOUT ELÆ [LYNNE DESILVA-JOHNSON]

ELÆ [Lynne DeSilva-Johnson] is a multimodal creative practitioner, cultural scholar and educator. Their work employs relational aesthetics, text, installation, sound design, performance, digital tech and speculative theory in addressing the somatic, ontological intersections between persons, forms of language, and systems, as well as the study of resilient, open source strategies for ecological and social change. Recent and forthcoming features include Protagony at The Exponential Festival, How to Human: Resistance Protocols as part of Performing Knowledge at the Segal Center, the Speculative Resilience Radical Practice Library & Lab for the Anarchist Bookfair, Dixon Place's HOT! Festival, and an onsite field lab installation for bioart/AI collaborative team APRIORI at Ars Electronica / STWST 2019. Recent and forthcoming publications include *Vestiges, Big Echo, Matters of Feminist Practice, The Transgender Narratives Anthology, Choice Words: Writers on Abortion*, and many more. They are the creator of many publication projects including *Ground, Blood Altas, Overview Effect*, and the forthcoming *Sweet and Low: Indefinite Singular*. Collaborative publications include *Boddy Oddy Oddy*, an ekphrastic project with painter Georgia Elrod, and *The Collaborative Precarity Bodyhacking Work-Book and Guide*, with Cory Tamler and Storm Budwig. They are a Visiting Assistant Professor at Pratt Institute, as well as a frequent facilitator for workshops in schools and community organizations. They curate and host events regularly in New York and elsewhere, and are the Founder/Creative Director of The Operating System / Liminal Lab, Communications Manager at +More Art, as well as lead R&D for the Brooklyn node of the Mycelium Network Society. Use this door to their rhizomatic links on IG: @ thetroublewithbartleby

*The Operating System uses the language "print document" to differentiate from the book-object as part of our mission to distinguish the act of documentation-in-book-FORM from the act of publishing as a backwards-facing replication of the book's agentive *role* as it may have appeared the last several centuries of its history. Ultimately, I approach the book as TECHNOLOGY: one of a variety of printed documents (in this case, **bound**) that humans have invented and in turn used to archive and disseminate ideas, beliefs, stories, and other evidence of production.*

Ownership and use of printing presses and access to (or restriction of printed materials) has long been a site of struggle, related in many ways to revolutionary activity and the fight for civil rights and free speech all over the world. While (in many countries) the contemporary quotidian landscape has indeed drastically shifted in its access to platforms for sharing information and in the widespread ability to "publish" digitally, even with extremely limited resources, the importance of publication on physical media has not diminished. In fact, this may be the most critical time in recent history for activist groups, artists, and others to insist upon learning, establishing, and encouraging personal and community documentation practices. Hear me out.

With The OS's print endeavors I wanted to open up a conversation about this: the ultimately radical, transgressive act of creating PRINT /DOCUMENTATION in the digital age. It's a question of the archive, and of history: who gets to tell the story, and what evidence of our life, our behaviors, our experiences are we leaving behind? We can know little to nothing about the future into which we're leaving an unprecedentedly digital document trail — but we can be assured that publications, government agencies, museums, schools, and other institutional powers that be will continue to leave BOTH a digital and print version of their production for the official record. Will we?

As a (rogue) anthropologist and long time academic, I can easily pull up many accounts about how lives, behaviors, experiences — how THE STORY of a time or place — was pieced together using the deep study of correspondence, notebooks, and other physical documents which are no longer the norm in many lives and practices. As we move our creative behaviors towards digital note taking, and even audio and video, what can we predict about future technology that is in any way assuring that our stories will be accurately told – or told at all? How will we leave these things for the record?

In these documents we say:
WE WERE HERE, WE EXISTED, WE HAVE A DIFFERENT STORY

- Elæ [Lynne DeSilva-Johnson], Founder/Creative Director
THE OPERATING SYSTEM, Brooklyn NY 2018

DOC U MENT
/däkyəmənt/

First meant "instruction" or "evidence," whether written or not.

noun - a piece of written, printed, or electronic matter that provides information or evidence or that serves as an official record
verb - record (something) in written, photographic, or other form
synonyms - paper - deed - record - writing - act - instrument

[*Middle English, precept, from Old French, from Latin documentum, example, proof, from docre, to teach; see dek- in Indo-European roots.*]

Who is responsible for the manufacture of value?

Based on what supercilious ontology have we landed in a space where we vie against other creative people
in vain pursuit of the fleeting credibilities of the scarcity economy, rather than freely collaborating
and sharing openly with each other in ecstatic celebration of MAKING?

While we understand and acknowledge the economic pressures and fear-mongering
that threatens to dominate and crush the creative impulse, we also believe that
now more than ever we have the tools to relinquish agency via cooperative means,
fueled by the fires of the Open Source Movement.

**Looking out across the invisible vistas of that rhizomatic parallel country we can begin to see our community
beyond constraints, in the place where intention meets resilient, proactive, collaborative organization.**

Here is a document born of that belief, sown purely of imagination and will.
When we document we assert. We print to make real, to reify our being there.
When we do so with mindful intention to address our process, to open our work to others, to create beauty
in words in space, to respect and acknowledge the strength of the page we now hold physical, a thing in our hand,
we remind ourselves that, like Dorothy: *we had the power all along, my dears.*

THE PRINT! DOCUMENT SERIES
is a project of
the trouble with bartleby
in collaboration with
the operating system